Stearns & Benton Counties
The First 100 Years

Presented by the *St. Cloud Times* in conjunction with
the Stearns History Museum and Benton County Historical Society

ACKNOWLEDGEMENTS

The *St. Cloud Times* would like to thank the staff and volunteers of the Stearns History Museum and the Benton County Historical Society for the many hours of photo collection and information they verified in putting together this book. Many of the photographs are reprinted here courtesy of the Stearns History Museum and Benton County Historical Society.

In addition, we would like to extend a special thank you to the many central Minnesota residents who shared their treasured family photographs. They are an irreplaceable resource in recording the history and heritage of Stearns and Benton counties in the early years.

We would also like to recognize the efforts of Connie Matz for the invaluable contributions she made to this publication. Additionally, special thanks to Marion Gross, Joel Rohlik, Celeste Simon, Bill Albrecht, Mike Corbett and Dennis Host for their work in producing this book.

Every effort has been made to identify as many individuals as possible in the photographs included in this book.

This book has been made possible by the generous support of the

www.sctimes.com

Copyright© 2002 • ISBN: 1-932129-18-9

All rights reserved. No part of this book may be reproduced, stored in a retrieval system or transmitted in any form or by any means, electronic, mechanical, photocopying, recording or otherwise, without prior written permission of the copyright owner or the publisher.

Published by Pediment Publishing, a division of The Pediment Group, Inc.   www.pediment.com   Printed in Canada

Table of Contents

FOREWORD 4

SCENES 5

   HOME AND FAMILY 11

   RELIGION 26

   EDUCATION 34

SOCIETY 51

   PUBLIC SERVICE 58

   COMMERCE 70

   INDUSTRY AND AGRICULTURE 84

   TRANSPORTATION 98

   SPORTS AND LEISURE 109

   EVENTS 122

Foreword

Granite quarrying. Agriculture. Amateur baseball. The 1886 tornado. These are just a few of the countless factors and significant events that helped Stearns and Benton counties emerge into what we know them to be today.

With the establishment of these two counties in 1856, this book serves as a passage through their first 100 years. Life in Central Minnesota depicted through these priceless photographs.

This book is not intended to be a comprehensive record of the development of Stearns and Benton counties. Rather it is meant to serve as a visual remembrance of our proud heritage. Or perhaps it is best defined as a glimpse at the hardships these settlers faced, the struggles they endured and the tremendous successes they achieved at founding their towns, establishing their businesses and industries, and living their lives in Central Minnesota.

We are proud to bring you *Stearns and Benton Counties – The First 100 Years*.

Bill Albrecht
President and Publisher
St. Cloud Times

SCENES

Lower town, St. Cloud, 1877. *Courtesy Stearns History Museum 8713*

The serenity and remote beauty of an isolated farm, its crops and meadows nestled in the countryside. Fields plowed by dedicated farming families who worked their land in the hope of reaping plentiful harvests.

The main streets of downtown St. Cloud and Sauk Rapids complete with horse drawn carriages and Model T Ford automobiles…streets lined with small shops run by proud proprietors, frequented by townspeople and country folk alike. As these communities began to flourish, it was the strength of the people who settled here who worked hard to contribute to the growth of their local economy.

Serving as a quiet backdrop, the Mississippi River was a witness to the evolution of Stearns and Benton counties. The river lies at the heart of this expansion.

Communities grew despite many struggles. Harsh climates would pose major challenges with bitter cold winters and unrelenting humid summers.

However the resolve of early settlers working to establish permanence of their communities would prove successful. Neighborhoods grew, smaller towns like Richmond and St. Joseph emerged and flourished. The landscape of Stearns and Benton counties evolved into areas of great industrial and residential growth.

East Main Street in Sauk Rapids, circa 1900. *Courtesy Benton County Historical Society 722*

5th Avenue in St. Cloud viewed from the southwest corner of 1st Street South, circa 1905. *Courtesy Stearns History Museum 1809*

North side of the 500 block, St. Germain Street, St. Cloud, 1907. *Courtesy Stearns History Museum 1752*

600 block of St. Germain Street looking east, circa 1910. *Courtesy Stearns History Museum 9244*

Main Street, Richmond, circa 1912. *Courtesy Stearns History Museum 12,695*

Aerial view of St. Joseph from the water tower, circa 1912. *Courtesy Stearns History Museum 12,413*

600 block of St. Germain Street looking west, circa 1916. *Courtesy Stearns History Museum 1761*

Downtown Foley, April 8, 1919. Cars gathered on the main street to transport Foley men who were drafted into service. *Courtesy Benton County Historical Society*

900 block of St. Germain Street looking east, 1929. *Courtesy Stearns History Museum 1799*

Gateway sign at St. Germain Street and Lincoln Avenue looking north, 1923. *Courtesy Stearns History Museum 10251*

Aerial view of St. Cloud looking southeast, circa 1934. *Courtesy Stearns History Museum 12,998*

Home & Family

People moved to Stearns and Benton counties to begin a new life, start a family, own a home, operate a farm. People like Mary Dombrovski, one of the area's first settlers in the early 1860s.

Settlers established roots, and with perseverance and pride, new generations emerged in the developing communities. Settlers who became proprietors, landowners, educators, or farmers. As a result, the area began to flourish, neighborhoods were formed, and churches were established.

The family served as the backbone for creating these new communities. The roles played by mothers and fathers, sisters and brothers, grandparents and grandchildren were vital to the overall success of Stearns and Benton counties. As pupils, congregations, workers, and farmers, the settlers' presence assured the potential for civic and economic expansion. Schools, churches and businesses were dependent upon the existence and growth of area families.

Extended families were often the norm in Central Minnesota households as well as families comprised of several children, as many of these archived photos indicate.

Family gathered at the Mike Pfannenstein home on Second Avenue Southwest in St. Joseph, circa 1915. Top row, left to right: Mary, Mike (Butch), Edward, Clara, John, Gertrude, Aloys, and George, Jr. Front row: Margaret, Martin, George, Sr., Daniel, Barbara, Frances, and Leona. *Courtesy Stearns History Museum 14,218*

The Joseph Blau home in Minden Township was built around 1900 near Christ Church in Minden. In buggy: Joseph and Karoline Blau and their daughter, Jannah. Henry Blau is standing next to the horse. Mrs. Minnie Blau is on the porch holding Martha. Children in front: Eric, Henry, and Freida. Mrs. Robert Blau is holding Joseph, and the man on the far right is Robert Blau. *Courtesy Benton County Historical Society 437*

HOME & FAMILY ❖ Page 13

Mary McGregor, the daughter of Maybelle McGregor, married Erwin Walstedt of Sauk Rapids, circa 1900. *Courtesy Benton County Historical Society 896*

Hohmann farm buildings located southwest of St. Cloud, circa 1900. *Courtesy Stearns History Museum 2818*

The Mayman's residence on 2nd Street North in Sauk Rapids, circa 1900. *Courtesy Benton County Historical Society*

The Bechtold children outside their home in St. Joseph, circa 1910. Their parents were Frank X. and Magdalen Bechtold. Left to right: John, Frank, Joe, Martin, Peter, Albert, Hildegard, Cornelia, Cecelia, Catherine, Appolonia, and Rose. *Courtesy Lucy Bechtold*

Henry and Margaret Pramann family, 1900. Back row, left to right, Emelia, John, Henry, and Edward. Middle row: Henry's mother Johanna, Henry, and Margaret holding Fred. Front row: Adolph, Augusta, Anna, William, and George. *Courtesy Lavina Hoemke and Luilla Pelzer*

Henry Briol's wedding group at his bride's home, Albany, circa 1905. *Courtesy Stearns History Museum 13,476*

John Henry Lunemann with his wife, Augusta Miller Lunemann, and two of their three sons, John Miller and Roger Alan. They moved to East St. Cloud in 1913. John Henry died two years later at age 44. *Courtesy Rev. Duane Lunemann*

Guests at the wedding of Julia Murphy and Alex Stewart at her home in Brockway Township on February 9, 1915. *Courtesy Michael D. Murphy*

Weber-Garding gathering at Nick Weber's home in St. Martin Township, circa 1910. *Courtesy Stearns History Museum 14,500*

Joseph Netter holding Christine and his wife Martha holding Florence on Martha's parents farm in Foley, 1921. *Courtesy Dannielle Bunting*

Front row, left to right: Mrs. Mike Lorenz, unknown, and Tessie Lorenz Deen. Back row: George Yager and Ed Yager. They are pictured on the lawn of the Yager farm in rural St. Joseph, circa 1910. *Courtesy Alice Holmes*

Grandchildren of John Kotowski at his home at 15th Avenue and 3rd Street North in St. Cloud, circa 1914. In front are Raymond Ziebol and Eugene Kotowski. Robert Ziebol is in back. Martha Kotowski is sitting on the step in the background. *Courtesy Gloriann Ziebol*

Michael Kremer farm home, Luxemburg Township, circa 1904. Left to right: Margaret Neis, Louise in buggy, Frank, Michael, Sr., Rose, unknown, Mrs. Kremer, and Michael, Jr. *Courtesy Stearns History Museum 11,016*

Wedding of Taufen, bride, and Kuebelbeck, groom, on County Road 2 between St. Joseph and Cold Spring, circa 1910. *Courtesy Carole Sauer*

Mary Dombrovski, born in 1824, was one of the first settlers to the area in the early 1860s. She and her husband Jacob lived on the south side of St. Cloud. She lived to be 92 years old. *Courtesy Mary and Roger Dombrovski*

Mathilda, left, and her sister Kate Weihs on the steps of their home in St. Cloud, circa 1912. *Courtesy Mary and Roger Dombrovski*

Harold and Evelyn Hoemke, 1923, at their home on 24th Avenue North in St. Cloud. *Courtesy Lavina Hoemke*

Rose and Clara Pekarek in Alberta Township, 1921. *Courtesy Dorrain Petron*

A Sunday gathering at the Searle's Farm on Long Lake, rural Cold Spring, circa 1928. Back row, left to right: Otto Linz, John Albers, Joe Albers, Henry Albers, Joe Athman, Catherine and William Albers, Frank Eder holding an unknown child, Frank Albers, Bill Albers, Frank Linz, Fred Albers, and Cyril Albers. Middle row: Anna Linz holding Marion, Clara Linz, Anna Albers holding Florence, Mary Athman holding Lydia, Johanna Eder holding an unknown child, Catherine Albers, Frances Kremers holding Stella, and Ted Kremers holding Ted. Front row, children: Edmund Linz, Beatrice Linz, Cordelia Linz, Marietta Athman, Mathilda Athman, Rita Athman, Julia Athman, Geraldine Linz, Rudy Athman, Ray Linz, Richard Athman, Herb Athman, and Melvin Linz. *Courtesy Jerome and Joan Beckers*

Construction of a home on the corner of 8th Street North and 32nd Avenue North in St. Cloud, 1918. This was one of the homes built by the Pan Motor Company for its employees, 1918. *Courtesy Mildred Burnett*

A Pan Motor Company home being built on 31st Avenue North in Pantown in 1918. Samuel C. Pandolfo built these homes for his company employees. The area became known as Pantown. *Courtesy Mildred Burnett*

810 2nd Avenue North in Sauk Rapids, circa 1915. Left to right: Alda Hellum, Alda Fletcher, and William Fletcher, son of the builder of the house. *Courtesy Benton County Historical Society*

James and Sally Pekarek farmhouse in Alberta Township, 1944. *Courtesy Dorrain Petron*

HOME & FAMILY ❖ Page 21

John Schibilla family in front of their 1916 Model T, circa 1922. Front row, left to right: Verna, Florence, and Ambrose. On far right is Katherine Schibilla holding Herbert. In middle is Cecelia. Behind her is Al and Gert is in the communion dress. *Courtesy Arnold Patrias*

Grandchildren of William and Emma Gatzke on their farm in Linden Township, 1927. Left to right: Harold Hoemke, Marian Gatzke, Evelyn Hoemke, Luella Gatzke, and Melvin Gatzke. *Courtesy Lavina Hoemke*

Left to right are: Alice Thielman, cousin Ann Merkling, and Oswald Thielman, circa 1935, on the Thielman farm in Collegeville. *Courtesy S. Elaine Schroeder, OSB*

St. Cloud north-end neighborhood kids in front of the Dombrovski's 1934 Oldsmobile. Back row, left to right: Daniel Dombrovski, Marvin Dombrovski, Dorothy Zlock, and Harold Dombrovski holding Roger Dombrovski. Front row: Dick Brown, Vivian Dombrovski, Gladys Brown, Jim Dombrovski, Beverley Brown, Hub Dombrovski, and Evelyn Dombrovski. *Courtesy Mary and Roger Dombrovski*

Duane Lunemann at his family's home in St. Cloud, 1936. *Courtesy Rev. Duane Lunemann*

Roger Dombrovski, age 6, in the back yard of his family home on 18th Avenue in St. Cloud. *Courtesy Mary and Roger Dombrovski*

Elmer Stein, Sam Wenstrom, and Al Stein sitting left to right on a brand new Indian Motorcycle in 1937 at the back door of the Wenstrom home, 140 10th Avenue North, Waite Park. *Courtesy Sam Wenstrom*

The Netter children, 1926. Left to right: Florence, Felix, and Christine holding Helen. *Courtesy Dannielle Bunting*

John Albers and his children Duane and Joan on the running board of his 1934 Chevrolet. *Courtesy Joan Beckers*

Wolters children with their parents' Ford at their home in St. Cloud, circa 1942. Left to right: Melvin, Patricia, Kenneth, and Alice. *Courtesy Corinne C. Klemz*

Ellen and Louis Holmes with their children, Calvin and Edward, 1928. The Holmes lived in St. Cloud. *Courtesy Alice Holmes*

Margaret Wolters holding her daughter, Alice, and a neighbor, Mrs. Dockedorf, in Rockville, 1938. *Courtesy Corinne C. Klemz*

Claude and Loretta Dullinger with their daughter Carole in front of their home in St. Cloud, 1942. *Courtesy Carole Sauer*

Ben and Alice Schroeder with their girls, Mary Alice and Elaine, on their homestead north of Richmond, 1942. *Courtesy S. Elaine Schroeder, OSB*

Theodor Ritsche and Agnes Leyendecker at Stearns County Courthouse to obtain their marriage license in 1933. They are standing in front of Theodor's first car, a 1928 Pontiac with a rumble seat. *Courtesy Emilie Ritsche Trushenski*

Herman and Pauline Sand Krushek on their wedding day, April 22, 1941. Their wedding dance was at the New Munich Coliseum with music provided by Jerry Dostal and his Orchestra. *Courtesy Maynard Sand*

Three Moehrle siblings married three Schramel siblings. Parents of the Moehrles are the older couple in the front, Mary and Martin. Their son Joe Moehrle and his wife Margaret Schramel are in the back on the left. Their daughter Louise Moehrle and her husband Marcus Schramel are in the back to the right of their parents. Their daughter Christine Moehrle and her husband John Schramel are on the far right. The children in front, left to right: Bernadine, Joanne, Joe, Jr., Mary Lou, Martin, and Joe. *Courtesy Emilie Ritsche Trushenski*

Rita Salaski at a wedding at the St. Joseph Catholic Church in Waite Park, seen in background. The car is a 1940 Chevrolet. *Courtesy Rita Osgood-Klein*

Dr. and Mrs. John Yager, Christmas of 1941. John and his brother George were both veterinarians. *Courtesy Alice Holmes*

Margaret Wolters with her son Melvin, circa 1948. Melvin served in the Navy during WW II aboard the U.S.S. Coral Sea. *Courtesy Corinne C. Klemz*

HOME & FAMILY ❖ Page 25

Sam Wenstrom, age five, sits on a 1937 Indian motorcycle in the driveway of the Wenstrom home, 140 10th Avenue North. His father sold and serviced cars and motorcycles in his Waite Park garage from the early 1920s to 1939. *Courtesy Sam Wenstrom*

John Sand, Maynard Sand, and Ted Thull on their First Communion, 1937. The ceremony was in the Immaculate Conception Church in New Munich. This photo was taken on the Leo Sand farm in St. Martin township. *Courtesy Maynard Sand*

Carol Joan Reinke, right, and Penny Lee Reinke, left, in 1945 following the Back-To-School Parade sponsored by the St. Cloud Chamber of Commerce. They won a grand prize of $10 for their Miss America float. *Courtesy Irene Reinke*

Jackie Lutgen's birthday party, first grade, at her home at 14th Avenue South in St. Cloud, 1944. Back row, left to right: Leila Athman, Joan Albers, and Dorine Peerman. Front row: Jackie Lutgen, unknown, Renee Borgert, Pat Johnson, and Mary Kay Nilan. *Courtesy Jerome and Joan Beckers*

RELIGION

Religion plays a vital role in the heritage of Stearns and Benton counties. The area boasts a rich tradition of religious observance and spirituality.

For some of its early settlers, the freedom to practice their religion in peace must have proved a major factor in deciding to relocate to Central Minnesota.

One of the strongest displays of faith a community can demonstrate is the establishment of a church. As churches were established they not only signified the pride of its congregation but also their resolve in creating a place to worship, a place to find peace, a place to turn to throughout life's struggles. The churches of Stearns and Benton counties also served as landmarks, places that represented the spirit and determination of the first people who chose to call Central Minnesota home.

The importance of religion not only inspired settlers to build churches, it also emerged in many of the area's early schools.

The establishment of churches and religious schools allowed people to strengthen their beliefs, to continue their traditions and practice their customs.

Cold Spring confirmation class at St. Boniface Catholic Church, circa 1907. Dan Oster is in the center, back row; others unidentified. *Courtesy Stearns History Museum 14,498*

RELIGION ❖ Page 27

Holy Angels Catholic Church interior, St. Cloud, 1893. The church was destroyed by fire in 1933. Courtesy Stearns History Museum 8140

Holy Cross Church, Marty (Pearl Lake), 1909. Courtesy Stearns History Museum 7415

The congregation of St. Patrick's Catholic Church of Minden Township in 1910. The church was built in 1880. *Courtesy Benton County Historical Society*

RELIGION ❖ Page 29

Officials from St. Cloud Diocese, circa 1900. Bishop James Trobec is fourth from the left with glasses; Reverend John Trobec is next to the right; others unidentified. *Courtesy Stearns History Museum 8139*

Sauk Rapids Congregational Church Ladies Aid, circa 1908. *Courtesy Benton County Historical Society 783*

Sauk Rapids Evangelical Lutheran School students in December, 1908. *Courtesy Benton County Historical Society 786*

St. Mary's Church and School, St. Cloud, 1907. The church was destroyed by a fire in 1920. *Courtesy Stearns History Museum 12,884*

St. John's Evangelical Lutheran Church of Popple Creek was dedicated on November 20, 1910, with three services: one in German, one English, one Polish. *Courtesy Benton County Historical Society*

St. James Catholic Church, Jacobs Prairie, circa 1910. *Courtesy Stearns History Museum 12,636*

Interior view of Sacred Heart Chapel, College of St. Benedict, St. Joseph. The Chapel was built from 1911-1914 and seated 500 people. *Courtesy Darol Studer*

St. Margaret's Church, Lake Henry, August, 1923. *Courtesy Stearns History Museum 14,425*

St. Joseph Catholic Church in Waite Park, circa 1930. *Courtesy Jerome and Joan Beckers*

Construction of the First Evangelical Church, 7th Avenue and 6th Street, St. Cloud, 1929. *Courtesy Lavina Hoemke*

First Communion class at St. Hedwig's Catholic Church, Holdingford, June 3, 1928. Fourth from the right in the back row is Verna Schibilla; others unidentified. *Courtesy Arnold Patrias*

Sacred Heart Rectory in Sauk Rapids, circa 1925. *Courtesy Benton County Historical Society*

Sauk Rapids Congregational Church choir, circa 1920. Left to right: Ruth Toppings, Harry Snavely, Dorthea Larson, Lester Snavely, Clara Olson, Mabel Edmond, Minnie Hurd, Vesta Potter, Sara Hurd, Mrs. Arensberger, Miss Carpenter, director Mrs. George Galley, Harry Olson, Jr. *Courtesy Benton County Historical Society 779*

Religion ❖ Page 33

Sixth grade confirmation class at St. Mary's grade school, St. Cloud, 1949. *Courtesy Joan Beckers*

EDUCATION

Schools played many roles in the lives of its students. Not only was teaching children the sufficiency to one day take on a family business or pursue further educational opportunities essential, but in many cases, school picnics, socials and field trips often provided rare opportunities for children to form relationships with one another outside the classroom. Getting to class could itself be a test of will as, in the instance of rural communities, schoolhouses were often located several miles from home and inclement weather would only exacerbate long distances.

While some of the class sizes were quite small, many others had numerous students with only one teacher to educate and discipline a room full of pupils.

Minnesota's third "Normal School" opened in 1869 and evolved into St. Cloud State University, whose heritage of academic excellence and opportunity now boasts an enrollment of nearly 15,000 students and is the state's second largest university.

Schools provided the first settlers of Stearns and Benton counties another form of community not only for themselves, but also establishing a sense of belonging for its children.

Graduating class of St. Clotilde's Academy of Music and Kindergarten, St. Cloud, circa 1900. Included are: Anna Trossen, Frances Renskin, Bertha Kropp, Katherine Keys, Louise Wimmer, Adelaide Dunn, John Chase, Arthur Gorman, Frank Beaudreau, and Robert Schaefer. *Courtesy Stearns History Museum 8,740*

St. Cloud Normal School, 1890. *Courtesy Stearns History Museum 8,278*

German Catholic Teachers Association convention at St. Martin, August, 1897. *Courtesy Stearns History Museum 11,341*

Sauk Centre Public School class, circa 1900. *Courtesy Stearns History Museum 7511*

A rural schoolhouse in Stearns County, May 26, 1905. *Courtesy Alice Holmes*

Russell School students, 1917. *Courtesy Benton County Historical Society 761*

Waite Park school children on the front steps of the school, April, 1906. Harold Wenstrom, standing in the top row, far left, was eight years old and in the second grade; others unidentified. *Courtesy Sam Wenstrom*

Red brick schoolhouse, District #117, Albany, circa 1905. J.A. Krause was the teacher. *Courtesy Stearns History Museum 13,477*

Holy Angels Catholic School first grade, St. Cloud, circa 1910. *Courtesy Stearns History Museum 8,184*

Primary class in Waite Park, circa 1912. *Courtesy Stearns History Museum 8,287*

Sauk Rapids Russell School, circa 1915. *Courtesy Benton County Historical Society 682*

Holy Angels Grade School graduating class, St. Cloud, circa 1905. Back row, left to right: Estella Eich, Amanda Quinlivan, Madeline Martin, Elsie Borck, Helen Brennan, Ellen Morrisson, and Clara Brennan. Second row: Olivia Weismann, Theresa Blommer, Marie Rosenberger, Clara Mockenhaupt, Elizabeth Hadersbeck, Monica Barthelemy, unknown, and Irene Danneker. Third row: Lena Hartel, Elizabeth Eizenhoefer, Mathilda Blommer, Ermalinda Kost, Louise Leonard, Elizabeth Prem, and Stella Roche. *Courtesy Stearns History Museum 8,741*

1917 Sauk Rapids graduates. Back row, left to right: Norb Berquist, Irene Pelton, Harry Burns, Bertha Blaske, and Pierre Hoskins. Middle row: Uena Orcutt, George Hagquist, Mabel Grunnewald, Marian Keller, Page Sartell, and Vesta G. Potter. Front row: Miss Cedarstrom, Charlotte Clifton, Ernest Larson, Marion Campbell, and Elsie Sliezer. *Courtesy Benton County Historical Society*

First class at the Albany High School, 1919. Standing, left to right: teacher and principal Harry Burns, Eleanor Brandtner, Ann Fruth, Lidwina Ohmann, Ray Krebs, and Elizabeth Dinndorf. Seated in middle row: Marie Christen, Adeline Bach, and Olivia Hanauer. Front: Elmer Winter, Mathilda Ohmann, Sabina Fox, and Hildegard Gretsch. *Courtesy Stearns History Museum 14,350*

CHS class on a field trip to a photography shop in 1918. *Courtesy Benton County Historical Society 8278*

Russell School fifth grade class of 1914. Teacher was Amelia Gerber. *Courtesy Benton County Historical Society*

St. Cloud State College with Old Main in the center of the photo, circa 1910. *Courtesy Stearns History Museum 8133*

Children at School District #38 in Graham Township. Back row, left to right: Margaret Petron, Clara Popp, unknown, Olga ___, and Rose ___. Front row: Alma, Millie Thoen, Sally Petron, Laura Stellmach, Josephine Popp, and Irene Kienow. 1922. *Courtesy Dorrain Petron*

Melrose High School, circa 1912. The school was built in 1903 by Melrose builder Ed C. Richmond. The school burned on March 21, 1914. *Courtesy Stearns History Museum 14,440*

Thoen School students in 1917. Thoen School was in District #38, Graham Township, Benton County. Elsie J. Murray was the teacher. Pupils included: Emmet Thoen, Vernon Thoen, Clara Popp, Thekla Popp, Katherine Popp, Louie Popp, Lorenz Popp, Emma Popp, Willie Popp, Helen Pietron, Margret Pietron, Ralph Pietron, Glen Jensen, Ralph Kienow, Aloys Van Den Hewel, Ethel Larsen, Edna Boelz, Walter Boelz, Lorenz Boelz, Harold Thoen, Alma Keske, Louisa Popp, Elenora Popp, Henry Popp, Clarence Popp, Julius Popp, Rose Popp, Anton Popp, Alice Pietron, Martina Pietron, Clair Jensen, Floyd Jensen, Ella Krause, Elra Larsen, Jennie Larsen, Olga Boelz, Clarence Boelz, and Emma Olson. J. M. Thoen served as clerk; F. J. Popp, treasurer; and Frank Pietron, director. *Courtesy Thomas Boelz*

Graduating class of St. Cloud Technical High School, 1918. J. Miller Lunemann is in the back row, far right. Miss Elizabeth Clark, principal, in the second row, far right, was principal until 1947-48. Others are unidentified. *Courtesy Rev. Duane Lunemann*

School District #38 in Graham Township, circa 1920. Included in picture: Frank Popp; Clarence Popp; sitting on step is Ralph Petron; in the big dress is Alma Keske; Laura Stellmach; Sally Petron; Josephine Popp; John Popp; Ray Boelz; and Elizabeth Popp. *Courtesy Dorrain Petron*

Classroom in rural St. Wendel Township, circa 1925. Seated second from the right is Alice Thielman; others unidentified. *Courtesy S. Elaine Schroeder, OSB*

Alice Thielman's students at District #132 north of Richmond, circa 1935. *Courtesy S. Elaine Schroeder, OSB*

Eighth grade graduation, Albany, 1924. Arthur J. Harren is the second from the left in the front row; others unidentified. *Courtesy Arlene Harren*

Sauk Rapids High School class of 1937. *Courtesy Benton County Historical Society*

Kindergarten class from Wilson Elementary School in 1940. Roger Dombrovski is on the far right in the back row; others are unidentified. *Courtesy Mary and Roger Dombrovski*

First grade students at Jefferson Elementary School in St. Cloud buying war bond stamps in 1944. Front row, left to right: Marilyn Ziegler, teacher Miss Ingrid Field, Neil Zniewski, Patricia Lehman, Barbara Lehman, and Arlene Wischnewski. Back row: Carl Zniewski, David Nearman, Clarence Horman, Twyla Busse, Earl Zniewski, Max Benward, Donald Watkins, and Robert Horman. *Courtesy Arlene Wischnewski Harren*

Fifth grade class from the St. Mary's grade school, St. Cloud, 1947. Sister Ann Lorette, right, was their teacher and Sister Emily-Ann, left, was their music teacher. *Courtesy Joan Beckers*

Central Junior High School, 1949. The old building, Union School, was to the left. *Courtesy Rev. Duane Lunemann*

Miss Hill's third grade class at Jefferson Elementary School, 1946. Arlene Wischnewski is second from the front on the left; others unidentified. *Courtesy Arlene Wischnewski Harren*

Osauka sophomores of 1940-41. *Courtesy Benton County Historical Society*

Faculty of Central Junior High School, 1949. Back row, left to right: Ray Deneen, Fred Pomije, Art Johnson, Mac Doane, and Dewey Reed. Fourth row: Richard Winter, unknown, unknown, Florence Trochill, and Andy Anderson. Third row: Harold House, unknown, unknown, Adolph White, and Charles Stark. Second row: principal Miller Lunemann, Adeline Fedje, Regina Martini, unknown, unknown, John Sherber, and unknown. Front row: unknown, unknown, unknown, Angie Vuterecker, and unknown. *Courtesy Rev. Duane Lunemann*

SOCIETY

Involvement in civic organizations, church groups and visiting with neighbors were some ways people not only socialized but progressed, making their communities more productive, enjoyable places to live.

Weddings were an important event in early Central Minnesota society. The joyous event of matrimony was celebrated not only within the families of the bride and groom, but often with their respective communities.

Since many of the families of the time were quite large while the scope of the overall area's population was modest, it was not uncommon for two or three members from one family to marry members from another family. Or for siblings to marry their respective spouses in a shared ceremony, creating an extra special family celebration while no doubt saving a little money, such as the double wedding of Bertha Chapek and Joe Bible and Rose Chapek and John Zabloske in 1912.

Double wedding of John Zabloske and Rose Chapek and Bertha Chapek and Joe Bible on November 6, 1912.
Courtesy Arlene Patrias

Margaret Kronenberg and Henry Pramann wedding, September 27, 1883. *Courtesy grandchildren of Lavina Hoemke and Luilla Pelzer*

Wedding of George and Elizabeth Heim, November 20, 1893. Attendants were Anton Weisz, Anne Heim Zierden, John Heim, and Maggie Heim Langendorf. *Courtesy Eugene Fischer*

Wedding of John Roske and Rose Sowada, May 29, 1911. Back: Joseph Sowada, bride's brother; Rosalia Sowada, groom's sister; Joseph Roske, groom's brother; and Agnes Sowada, bride's cousin. *Courtesy Jerome and Joan Beckers*

Xavier Braun Family, 1902. Seated, left to right: Elizabeth, Xavier Braun, and Mrs. Braun. Standing: Gretchen, Frank, Mary, John, and Barbara. *Courtesy Eugene Fischer*

Walter and Elizabeth Murphy with their children. Back row, left to right: Mary, Walter, Jr., Eugene, and Rose. Front row: Elizabeth, Cecilia, George, and Walter. Walter was a railroad contractor much of his life and served as Chief of Police in St. Cloud in 1898. *Courtesy Michael D. Murphy*

Clara Eltrich and Mathew Fiala, Jr., on their wedding day, June 24, 1902. Attendants, back row, left to right: Kate Boerger, Mary Eltrich, Joseph Fiala, and Joseph Eltrich. *Courtesy Gloriann Ziebol*

Wedding of Peter Beckers and Elizabeth Euteneuer, October 1, 1912. Standing behind are Peter's brother and sister, John and Mary. *Courtesy Jerome and Joan Beckers*

Mary Ann Murphy and Dennis George Callahan on their wedding day, February 21, 1898. They settled on a farm in St. Wendel township. *Courtesy Michael D. Murphy*

Chapek family from Benton County near Foley, circa 1900. Back row, left to right: Mary, Bertha, Katherine, and Julia. Front row: Frank, Rose, and Katherine. *Courtesy Arlene Patrias*

Christine Nett Diedrich, circa 1885. She married Pancratius Diedrich in 1850. *Courtesy Ruth Litke*

Adam Langer, circa 1900. He started in St. Cloud as a wagon maker with a hotel in his house and in 1856 was one of the first to settle in LeSauk Township five miles north of St. Cloud. *Courtesy Ruth Litke*

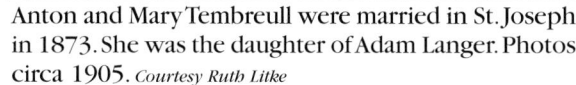

Anton and Mary Tembreull were married in St. Joseph in 1873. She was the daughter of Adam Langer. Photos circa 1905. *Courtesy Ruth Litke*

Edith Yager, daughter of Katherine and Adam Yager. She and her father were killed by a train on March 16, 1907, while driving a team of horses home from a butter and milk route in St. Cloud. Their death left Katherine alone to raise their remaining children which included a young set of triplets. Photo taken in 1907. *Courtesy Alice Holmes*

Hadersbeck family, 1912. Back row, left to right: Elizabeth, Robert, Mary, John, Frances, and Michael. Middle row: Josephine, Isadore, and Marie. Front row: Alfred, Joseph, and Ceil. *Courtesy Arlene Harren*

William and Catherine Albers family, 1914. Back row, left to right: Joe, Henry, Frank, Clara, Mary, and Anna. Second row: Johanna, Bill, and Fred. Front row: John, William, Katherine, Catherine, baby Cyril, and Frances. *Courtesy Jerome and Joan Beckers*

Augusta Lunemann founded Oak Hill Rest Home in 1936 with a woman physician from St. Paul, Dr. Tofte. *Courtesy Rev. Duane Lunemann*

Women of Foley, circa 1910. Back row, left to right: Mrs. Riley, unknown, Mrs. Peterman, Mrs. Jim Murray, Mrs. Odegard, Mrs. Miller, Mrs. Harmon Becker, Mrs. McGuire, and unknown. Middle row: Alice Latterell, Mrs. Clark Latterell, Mrs. McNulty, Mrs. Lena Linns, Mrs. Orcutt, and unknown. Child is ___ Peterman. Front row: Liz Barthelemy, Mrs. Kate Murphy, Belle Broding, Lonetta Latterell Cratly, and Claudia Latterell Dziuk. *Courtesy Benton County Historical Society*

The Gallus sisters, circa 1923. Back row, left to right: Agnes, Victoria, and Mary. Front row: Julia and Hattie. *Courtesy Rita Osgood-Klein*

Pete and Nettie Jedlicka and Mary and John Bialka, Gilman, circa 1915. *Courtesy Dorrain Petron*

John Schibilla, right, and Frank Przybilla, left, circa 1909. *Courtesy Arnold Patrias*

Julia Murphy and Alex Stewart on their wedding day, February 9, 1915. *Courtesy Michael D. Murphy*

The Hadersbeck sisters in 1914. Left to right in the back row are: Elizabeth, Ceil, Frances, Margaret, and Mary. Seated in the front is Josephine. *Courtesy Arlene Harren*

Children of George Leonard Boelz, Benton County, circa 1908. Back, left to right: George Leaman, William Fredrich, and Wesley Robert. Front: Lawrence John and Clarence Leonard. *Courtesy Thomas Boelz*

Mathilda Weihs on her Solemn Communion, circa 1920. *Courtesy Mary and Roger Dombrowski*

The triplets of Adam and Katherine Yager: Ellen Eva Laurtie, Ethel Emma Josephine, and Elma Michael Theodore. Born in a farmhouse in rural Stearns County on May 12, 1903, they were the youngest of twelve children. Ellen and Ethel lived a long life, but Elma died at age 2 after he and his sisters wandered away from a picnic and ate too many green apples. Although they all became ill, the girls survived. *Courtesy Alice Holmes*

The golden wedding of August and Adelheid Torborg in 1930. Left to right: Gerhardt Torborg, August's nephew; August; Lorraine Schaefer, grandchild; Adelheid; and Elizabeth Kammers, Adelheid's sister. The boy on the left is another grandchild; on the right is Harold Torborg, grandchild. *Courtesy S. Elaine Schroeder, OSB*

Alphonse and Rose Fischer family, circa 1945. Standing, left to right: Walter, Alma, Cyril, Leona, and Clarence. Seated: Alphonse, Ray, Rose, and Emil. The family farmed in Mayhew Lake on the first farm north of Esselman's General Store. *Courtesy Eugene Fischer*

Wedding photo of Henry and Sophie Schroeder on June 5, 1923. Their attendants were Mike Reitmeier, Sophie's brother, and Lizzie Schroeder, Henry's sister. They were married at St. Peter and Paul's Church in Richmond. *Courtesy S. Elaine Schroeder, OSB*

PUBLIC SERVICE

Stearns and Benton counties were not without their public servants. The area produced individuals who rose to civic duty and established local government complete with law enforcement officers, fire fighters, county officials, and postal workers. They embodied the very essence of their emerging community and dedicated themselves to making their towns safe and fair places to live. These were individuals who as proud citizens served in the United States Military and fought for their country's freedom. The very freedom we enjoy today.

County courthouses were erected and stood as representations of respect, protection and authority. They were buildings where law and order were upheld and justice was rendered.

The public servants of this time, some of whom are pictured in these pages, embodied the very essence of citizen responsibility. Their commitment to civic duty was the foundation for the sense of security we have come to depend on.

Melrose Fire Department in front of the fire hall, circa 1895. *Courtesy Stearns History Museum 8,678*

Courthouse in Foley, built in 1901, after a successful petition to move the county seat from Sauk Rapids to Foley. Courtesy Benton County Historical Society

Stearns County officers, 1876. Milton P. Noel, County Surveyor; James M. McKelvy, Judge of District Court; P. B. Kaiser, Superintendent of Schools; John Zapp, Register of Deeds; Mathias Mickley, Sheriff; Peter Brick, Judge of Probate; John Otteson, not an officer; Lee Cramb, Assistant Clerk of Court; Mathias Maus, County Treasurer; E. B. Strong, Clerk of Court; Barney Vossberg, County Auditor; and the man in the silk hat is unknown. *Courtesy Stearns History Museum 6934*

Sauk Rapids Courthouse was destroyed by a fire in 1915. Courtesy Benton County Historical Society 705

St. Cloud Fire Department responding to a fire alarm. The photo is taken on 7th Avenue North and 1st Street looking south, circa 1895. *Courtesy Stearns History Museum 1820*

Hook and Ladder, St. Cloud Fire Department, circa 1877. Left to right: John Hennemann, Bertus Mueller, Andrew Hennemann, Jr., unknown, unknown, unknown, L. A. Evans, T. D. Robertson, and unknown. *Courtesy Stearns History Museum 8969*

Sauk Rapids Post Office on Broadway in 1929. Left to right: William Baron, Emil Kuron. *Courtesy Benton County Historical Society 640*

Moving the old Post Office Building from 8th Avenue and St. Germain to its new location on 3rd Avenue and St. Germain in 1937. The building became the City Hall. Two horses pulled the building along 16 railroad tracks. *Courtesy James Gammell*

Laying the line for the fire hydrants from St. Joseph to St. Benedicts, circa 1920. *Courtesy Darol Studer*

PUBLIC SERVICE ❖ Page 65

Minnesota State Reformatory, circa 1930. *Courtesy Stearns History Museum 13,456*

Boy Scouts on 5th Avenue in St. Cloud, circa 1912. Dr. Burley was the scoutmaster. *Courtesy Stearns History Museum*

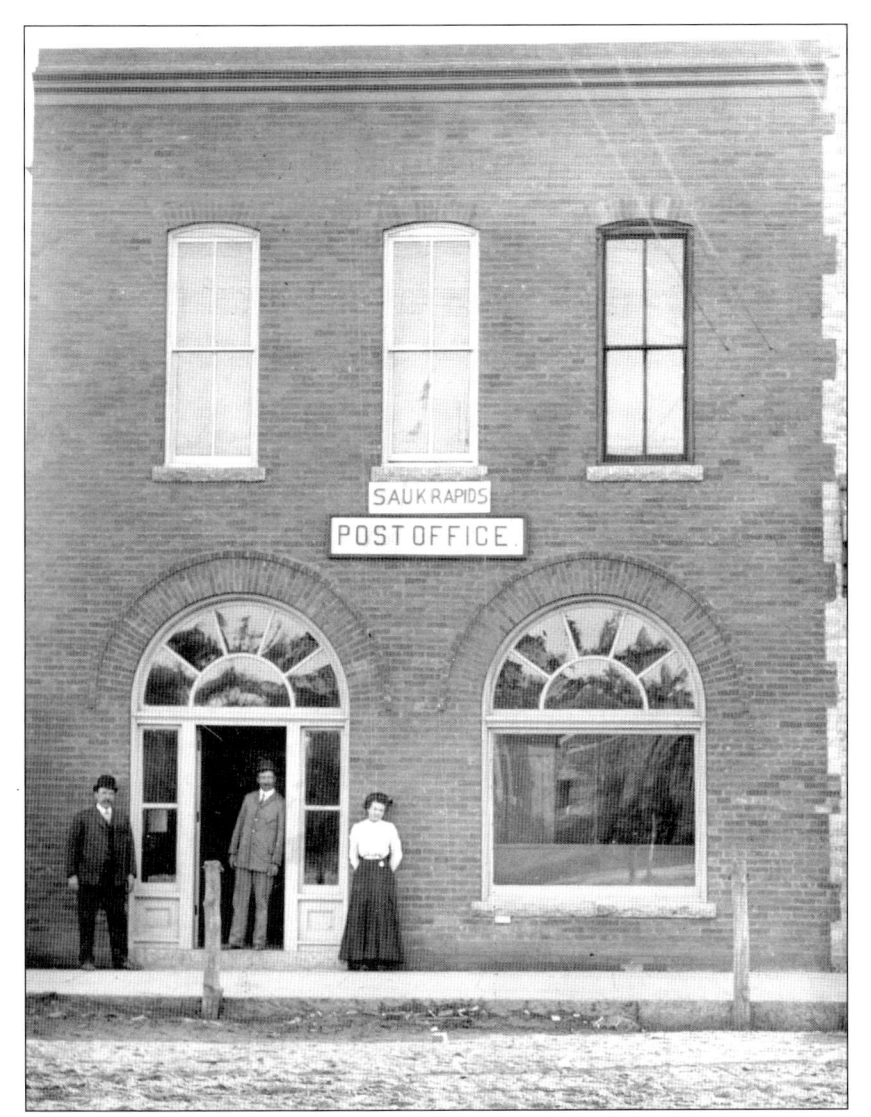

The first post office in Benton County was opened in Sauk Rapids in 1850. Peter Jensen is standing in the doorway; others unidentified. Photo is circa 1910. *Courtesy Benton County Historical Society 730*

Bryant Library, Sauk Centre, circa 1940. *Courtesy Stearns History Museum 12,317*

Dedication of a monument on Highway 15 on the day before Thanksgiving, 1949. The monument was made from two and one-half tons of Cold Spring granite and marked the spot where settlers from Maine established a community in 1856. *Courtesy Starns History Museum 1975*

World War I veterans of St. Joseph, 1919. Included in first row: Patty Weber, Nick Honsch, Joseph Pallansch, John Pallansch, Joseph Seitz, William Kuebelbeck, Ignatius Warnert, George Roeder, Celestine Meyer, Edward Pfannenstein, Fred H. Reber, and Frank Roeder. Second row, left to right: Joseph Warnert, Joseph Honsch, Aloys Pallansch, ___ Court, John Willeke, Louis Warnert, John Reber, Tony Willeke, Math Warnert, John Lauerman, George Warnert, Edward Linneman, Harry Hagen, unknown, and unknown. Included in third row: Frank Feichlinger, Pete Pallansch, Pete Lauerman, Leo Tobin, Joe Traut, and Herman Kremer. *Courtesy Stearns History Museum 8090*

Military funeral for Joseph "Smoke" Warnert, a WW I veteran, in St. Joseph, 1923. *Courtesy Darol Studer*

WW I soldiers at a Memorial Day service in St. Joseph, 1923. Second from right in front row is Fred Reber; others unidentified. *Courtesy Darol Studer*

Funeral for World War I veteran, John Lauerman, in St. Joseph, March 3, 1937. He was gassed in France during WW I. *Courtesy Darol Studer*

World War I veterans' Last Man's Party for Roy Martin, St. Cloud, 1940. Left to right: Paul Pappenfus, John Hanson, Gust Annis, Joe Sandkamp, Marcus Hengel, Hub Schmidt, Louis Rabe, and Roy Martin. *Courtesy Stearns History Museum 12,739*

Elks National Convention Chevrolet Magazine Tour Cars in front of the Elks building on 5th Avenue South in St. Cloud, circa 1937. *Courtesy Stearns History Museum 14,630*

Commerce

The need for provisions, communication and social interaction, and the dependence upon customers for economic health connected farmers and other rural homeowners with townsfolk. Many of the outlying area residents would travel to the downtown streets of St. Cloud or Sauk Rapids for food, supplies and services. Businesses relied on out-of-town customers who made the trips into town once a week or once a month as a healthy representation of their overall customer base.

Dry goods stores, clothing shops, drug stores, and hardware stores were some of the many businesses that provided an economic base for early Stearns and Benton counties. Hotels also provided another source of revenue as travelers visited the area and new settlers transitioned.

Population growth advanced the need for supermarkets, meat markets and bakeries. As the labor force expanded and people moved from rural areas to town, the demand for the convenience of restaurants and cafes emerged.

L. Thielman & Son hardware store, 703 Germain Street, circa 1895. *Courtesy Stearns History Museum 8864*

Central House, a St. Cloud hotel, 1877. *Courtesy Stearns History Museum 8876*

The Foley Hotel was built in the 1890s by the Foley brothers. In 1902 it was owned by County Sheriff Frank Leffingwell, who is in the buggy. *Courtesy Benton County Historical Society 17*

The Stearns House, circa 1870, St. Cloud's leading hotel in Civil War days, was at 8th Street South between 1st Avenue and the Mississippi River. It later became the men's dormitory for the Normal School. *Courtesy Stearns History Museum 1476a*

Belgrade Hotel, 1909. *Courtesy Stearns History Museum 234*

North side of the 500 block of St. Germain Street looking west in 1877. *Courtesy Stearns History Museum 1748*

Bensen Brothers Store on 5th Avenue in St. Cloud, circa 1900. Harry Bensen is second from the left and Edwin Bensen is third from the left. They were the sons of Mr. and Mrs. J. Andrew Bensen. *Courtesy Stearns History Museum 9,572*

Interior of Emerson-Hanson Drugstore, Sauk Centre, circa 1910. *Courtesy Stearns History Museum 7994*

John Bohnen's saloon, Freeport, March, 1930. John is behind the bar; customer unidentified. *Courtesy Stearns History Museum 13,237*

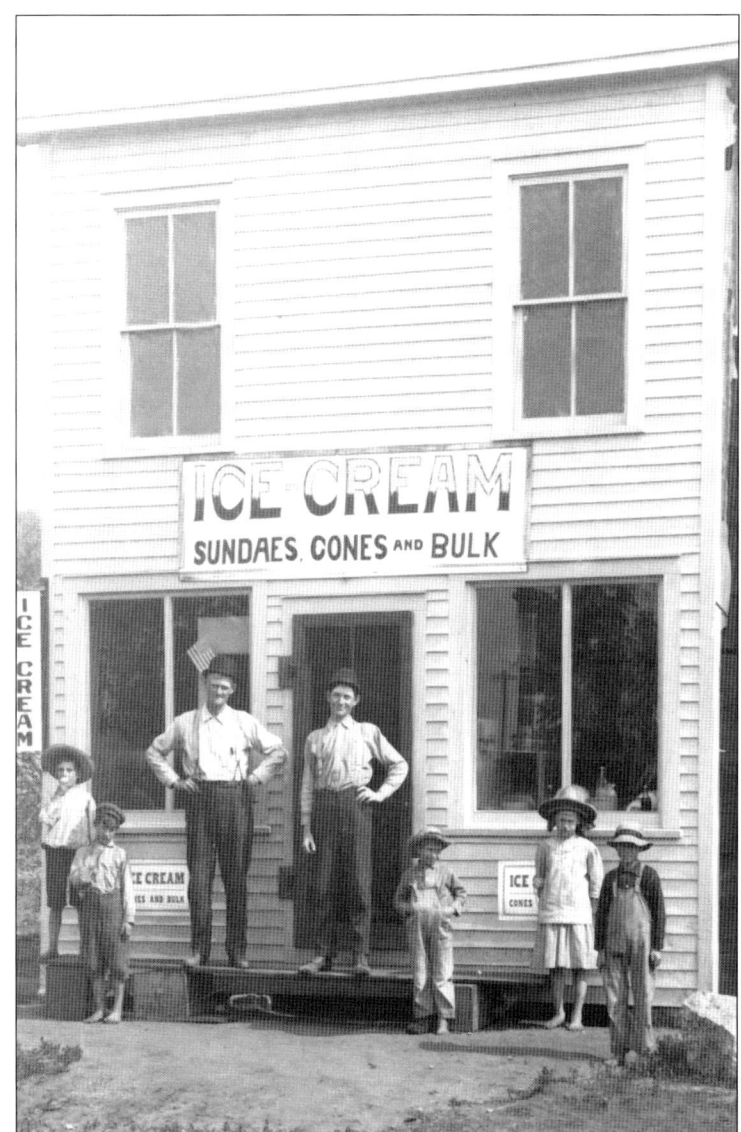

Charles Tenney Confectionary, Rockville, circa 1910. *Courtesy Stearns History Museum 12,024*

In 1883, Frank Fandel and Michael Nugent formed a partnership and purchased a dry goods business in St. Cloud. In 1895, Mr. Fandel purchased his partner's interest and became sole owner along with his sons. *Courtesy Stearns History Museum 8,662*

Sauk Rapids Hardware Store on the corner of Benton Drive and First Street South, circa 1920. Pictured are Joseph Neron, Marcel Steinbach, and Dominic Hennen. *Courtesy Benton County Historical Society 627*

Charles Heinzel Meat Market on the corner of South Broadway and Van Ness Street in Sauk Rapids, 1905. Left to right: Mrs. Frank Determan, unknown, August Heinzel, and Mrs. Goedker. *Courtesy Benton County Historical Society 629*

Heinzel Meat Market at the corner of South Broadway and Van Ness Street in Sauk Rapids, 1924. Left to right: Charles Heinzel, Paul Wickman, Eddie John, and August Heinzel. *Courtesy Benton County Historical Society 626*

Mike Cziok and Charles Reedstrom behind the counter of White Food Market in Sauk Rapids, 1920. *Courtesy Benton County Historical Society 625*

Interior of a St. Cloud bakery, 1930. Worker on the right behind the counter is Walter Wischnewski; others unidentified. *Courtesy Arlene Wischnewski Harren*

Interior of Hunstiger's Market at 117 5th Avenue South, 1925. Behind the counter are Anthony Hunstiger, owner, on the left and Jim Doerner, right. *Courtesy Stearns History Museum*

Sauk Rapids Hardware, circa 1915. *Courtesy Benton County Historical Society 630*

Sauk Rapids Hardware, circa 1925. *Courtesy Benton County Historical Society 728*

Falk Hardware and Furniture in Foley, circa 1920. *Courtesy Benton County Historical Society 361*

Interior of Fandel's Department Store, second floor, circa 1925. *Courtesy Stearns History Museum 13,070*

Home Maid Bakery on Broadway Avenue South in Sauk Rapids, 1940. *Courtesy Benton County Historical Society*

Dan's Lunch, the first hamburger shop owned by Red Schepers, right, and his partner George Steffes, at the corner of East St. Germain Street and Wilson Avenue in St. Cloud, 1931. *Courtesy Penny Bergtraser*

The Black and White hamburger shop owned by Red Schepers at the corner of East St. Germain Street and Wilson Avenue, 1933. *Courtesy Penny Bergtraser*

Bridget Schepers behind the counter at Red's Cafe, 411 East St. Germain Street, 1943. The cafe was owned by Emmett P. Schepers and his wife Bridget. *Courtesy Penny Bergtraser*

Steve Petrowske's Standard Station in Foley, circa 1930. *Courtesy Benton County Historical Society 220*

Industry & Agriculture

Early industries in Stearns and Benton counties included logging, blacksmith shops, milling, farming, and of course granite quarrying. The great Mississippi River not only enabled workers to transport logs to the sawmill, but the rock beneath the river bottom would become Central Minnesota's legacy.

Granite quarrying became the major industry in the area. Quarries were tapped for the great solid rock that would be used locally in the construction of buildings, bridges, for headstones and other monuments. Eventually granite quarried from Central Minnesota would be used on a national and even international scale.

Agriculture grew to become another major industry in Stearns and Benton counties. Farming was initially contained within one family who resided and worked on one piece of land. Families mainly subsisted on their own crops, livestock and vegetable gardens. Over the next several years, industrialization would revolutionize almost every type of labor including farming, revitalizing it into a business. Crops could now be planted and harvested on a much larger scale with the invention of tractors and threshing machines. Livestock sizes grew as farmers were now not only feeding their own families but were also producing a commodity.

Construction work on the dam near the paper mill at Sartell, 1907. *Courtesy Benton County Historical Society*

George Meyer is on left in front of his blacksmith shop and house in St. Joseph, circa 1910. *Courtesy Stearns History Museum 996*

Loggers at Pine Point just south of Gordon's Bridge in the 1880's. The logging was done from Pine Point in the winter and the logs were hauled over the ice to Sartell saw mill. *Courtesy Benton County Historical Society 703*

Workers at the Foley sawmill, circa 1910. Joe Freecheck is third from the left in the back row; others unidentified. *Courtesy Arlene Patrias*

Wood sawing near Rockville, circa 1910. *Courtesy Stearns History Museum 11,275*

Threshers at Robert Schulte farm in Albany, circa 1910. *Courtesy Stearns History Museum 1861*

Round barn near Duelm, circa 1900. *Courtesy Benton County Historical Society*

Round silo and feed shed on Rickmeyer farm in Fair Haven Township, circa 1900. *Courtesy Rachel Rickmeyer Bohm*

Threshing on the McNeal brothers' farm, circa 1910. On the right is a Case steamer. *Courtesy Benton County Historical Society*

INDUSTRY & AGRICULTURE ❖ Page 89

Foley Mill crew, circa 1910. Included are: Jim Kotsmith, Julius Popilek, Inatius Stahonius, Albert Latterell, John Kampa, F. J. Kampa, Leon Axtell, Ben Latterell, John Landowski, Charley Dziuk, Joe Kam, Emil Vanderkove, Perry Chase, and Charles Latterell. *Courtesy Benton County Historical Society*

Milton E. Merrill and his threshing rig, circa 1915. Mr. Merrill is standing on the tongue of the rig. *Courtesy Stearns History Museum 8,083*

Farmer's Milling Company Flour Mill, Cold Spring, circa 1915. *Courtesy Stearns History Museum 11,004*

Der Nordstern (newspaper) employees in front of St. Cloud Daily Times building, circa 1896. Nordstern papers with Royal Bake Soda ads on the first page appeared between October 10, 1895, and January 28, 1897. Adam Fischer, pressman, is second from the left. Gerhard May, editor, is the tall man in the middle. *Courtesy Stearns History Museum 14,407*

Sauk Rapids newspaper building, circa 1900. *Courtesy Benton County Historical Society 897*

Interior of Security Blankbook and Printing Company, St. Cloud, April 5, 1915. *Courtesy Stearns History Museum 8191*

Industry & Agriculture ❖ Page 91

Granite City Sign Company at 721 St. Germain Street in St. Cloud, circa 1908. *Courtesy Stearns History Museum 11,274*

Ignatius Kremer Cigar Factory, Cold Spring, circa 1910. Ignatius is second from the right. *Courtesy Stearns History Museum 9,749*

Fred and Tom Veenstra on the Whitney farm at Grand Lake, circa 1915. The Veenstras managed the farm for the Whitneys. *Courtesy Gloriann Ziebol*

Roman Peter Rassier on the Rassier farm in St. Wendel Township in 1916. They owned a 430-acre farm in Section 34 and 35. *Courtesy Michael D. Murphy*

George and Bertha Boelz family of Benton County, circa 1912. *Courtesy Thomas Boelz*

Andrew Pratschner working on the home farm in Albany, circa 1925. *Courtesy Arlene Harren*

Rex Granite Company on Lincoln Avenue Northeast in St. Cloud was founded in the 1920s by Axel Martinson. *Courtesy Benton County Historical Society*

Melrose Granite Company employees, St. Cloud, circa 1920. *Courtesy Stearns History Museum 10,366*

Industry & Agriculture ❖ Page 95

Granite City Bottling Works, St. Cloud, May, 1921. Pictured are Ben Junglen, John Knettel, Steve Justin, Charles A Bernick, Frank Justin, Adam Nickel, and Henry Knettel. *Courtesy Stearns History Museum 15,327*

Steam engine belonging to Bill Gatzke, Bill Koening, and Bill Weyrauch, circa 1930. *Courtesy Lavina Hoemke*

Andrew Pratschner working on the home farm in Albany, circa 1948. *Courtesy Arlene Harren*

George Prammann and his horses, Duke and Prince, on his farm in St. Augusta Township, 1947. *Courtesy Lavina Hoemke and Luilla Pelzer*

Building a barn on Martin Moehrle's farm. Martin and his brother Anton sponsored Theodor and Adolf Ritsche to come to the United States from Germany in 1923. Building Martin's barn was their first project. *Courtesy Emile Ritsche Trushenski*

Bernick's Dr. Pepper Bottling Company employees, 1946. Left to right: Jake Ruff, unknown, James Gammell, Red Diedrich, unknown, unknown, Ted Prom, Matt Jensen, and Art Ebnet. *Courtesy James Gammell*

Workers at the Donlin Millwork Company in East St. Cloud, 1942. Back row, left to right: third is Ted Ritsche, fifth is Bill Hartmann, eighth is Otto Hartmann, ninth is Paul Dlugosch, tenth is Jerry David. Front row: Fred Backus, George ___, Fritz Hartmann, unknown, and Gregor Dirschel. *Courtesy Emilie Ritsche Trusbenski*

Fleet of Megarry Bros. Trucks in front of International Harvester Co., East St. Cloud, circa 1935. *Courtesy Stearns History Museum 16,186*

TRANSPORTATION

Transportation took on many forms in early Stearns and Benton counties. People relied on horse-drawn wagons and buggies to get around town. Horses were used to plow and clear fields, haul supply loads and early on transported mail. Bridges and even a ferry system in the Clearwater-Clear Lake area enabled people to cross the Mississippi River and expand their communities.

The emergence of the United States rail system further revolutionized Central Minnesota. The railroad not only provided a better, more efficient method of travel, it created countless new jobs for track layers, rail operators, conductors, and later with the establishment of local depot stations, cashiers. Railroads not only connected the area in an entirely new way, it also connected Central Minnesota with the rest of the country.

Motorized cars soon emerged as the preferred method of travel, providing individuals with a new sense of freedom and adventure. And with the introduction of the automobile to the St. Cloud area came local auto manufacturer Samuel C. Pandolfo and his establishment of the Pan Motor Company.

An outing in their car near Richmond, circa 1912. Included are: Joe Viehauser, Pete Solinger, Mike Willenbring, Mary Viehauser Willenbring, and Irma Pappenfus. *Courtesy Stearns History Museum 12,478*

William Schultz with his horse hitched to his brother's new Sears Roebuck buggy, circa 1890. *Courtesy Stearns History Museum 931*

Clearwater ferry, which was run by Will Kirk, the man in the white shirt, circa 1910. *Courtesy Stearns History Museum 7011*

Wagon toll bridge at St. Germain Street looking southwest, circa 1870. *Courtesy Stearns History Museum 13,109*

T. Halvorson's grading crew in rural Albany, circa 1905. *Courtesy Stearns History Museum 13,474*

Richmond railroad station, circa 1912. Third from left is Peter J. Ganzer II, fourth from left is Alois 'Curly' Lang, fifth is railroad agent Henry C. Scharver (in white shirt), and on far right is ___Patonivich. *Courtesy Stearns History Museum 14,442*

Railroad crew in Foley, circa 1900. Joe Freecheck is sitting second from the right; others unidentified. *Courtesy Arlene Patrias*

Holdingford Depot, circa 1915. *Courtesy Darol Studer*

Streetcar that ran between Sauk Rapids, St. Cloud, and Waite Park, circa 1915.
Courtesy Stearns History Museum 7029

Street car on St. Germain Street looking west from 5th Avenue, circa 1918. *Courtesy Stearns History Museum 6745*

Bob and Mrs. Davidson on the bridge north of Rockville in their Morgan car, circa 1919. *Courtesy Stearns History Museum 12,623*

Left to right: Frank McGregor, passenger Bob Cross, driver Fred Sova, Harry Greimmen, and Dan Craig in a 1914 Ford. *Courtesy Benton County Historical Society 895*

Schlough Garage in Sauk Rapids, circa 1915. Left to right: Fermie Arensberger, Barney Deppa, Bell Kosloske, and Eleanor Sartell. *Courtesy Benton County Historical Society*

August and Tillie Bohm with their new Overland Touring car, circa 1915. The photo was taken at their home at 425 2nd Avenue Northeast. *Courtesy Roger Bohm*

Bako Process Auto Painting Co., O. R. 'Rudy' Strand, proprietor, 1925. The business was on the third floor of the St. Cloud Laundry, 116 1/2 5th Avenue South before moving in 1933 to 112 6th Avenue South. *Courtesy Lois Lunemann*

C. F. Brigham, Jr., Agnes Brigham, Kate Brigham, and Richard Colbert in a 1918 Buick on St. Germain Street, 1922. *Courtesy Stearns History Museum 14,105*

Isadore Schwinghammer going home from Benton County Fair in East St. Cloud, circa 1920. Bert Schwinghammer is on the hood of the truck. *Courtesy Stearns History Museum 1046*

Albert Fiala, in middle, at work in the Great Northern yards in St. Cloud, circa 1925. Others unidentified. *Courtesy Gloriann Ziebol*

Model T Ford, 1923. Riding in the back seat is Augusta Lunemann. Pretending to drive is her son Roger. Standing is son Mark, a bus starter for the Raymond Bus Company in St. Cloud. He would stand on the corner of Main Street and 7th Avenue in front of Metzroth's Clothing Store and explain the bus schedule. *Courtesy Rev. Duane Lunemann*

Richard Leyendecker by the 1928 Pontiac owned by his brother-in-law, Theodor Ritsche, 1933. *Courtesy Emilie Ritsche Trusbenski*

Arnold Patrias with a 1932 Chevrolet, 1939. *Courtesy Arnold Patrias*

Louis Patrias changing the tire on a 1936 Plymouth while his son, Arnold, and an unidentified man look on, 1940. *Courtesy Arnold Patrias*

Roger Dombrovski in front of his family's 1936 Oldsmobile at their home at 18th Avenue North, 1941. *Courtesy Mary and Roger Dombrovski*

Radio Cab owned by Clarence J. Witschen, 1949. He also owned Radio Wrecker Service. *Courtesy Dick Witschen*

Radio Wrecker Service owned by Clarence J. Witschen, 1949. He also owned Radio Cab. *Courtesy Dick Witschen*

James Gammell with his Miro Products van in 1949, which he bought for $500. He sold cleaning, finishing, and maintenance products door to door in St. Cloud. *Courtesy James Gammell*

August Bohm's 1940 Ford Deluxe purchased from Tenvoorde's for about $800. Photo is taken at their home at 419 2nd Avenue Northeast. *Courtesy Roger Bohm*

Jerome 'Romie' Beckers on his Whizzer bike, circa 1949. *Courtesy Jerome and Joan Beckers*

A crowd at the dedication of the St. Cloud airport on June 30, 1935. *Courtesy Stearns History Museum 11345*

Sports & Leisure

A rich, vibrant part of Central Minnesota's history was the enjoyment of sporting events, hobbies and arts and leisure activities. Through their competitive endeavors and performances local athletes, sportsmen and musicians brought excitement, amusement, culture, and entertainment to Stearns and Benton counties.

Amateur baseball teams helped provide a sense of camaraderie as their fellow townspeople rooted for their respective teams. Baseball teams were founded in several Central Minnesota towns. They played a major role as they nurtured and preserved hometown pride, fueled healthy competition and brought the simple enjoyment of what would become America's favorite pastime to area residents.

City bands were another important part of life's leisure side. The bands proudly represented their towns as festive participants in concerts, local parades and other civic celebrations, such as the July 4th, 1895 performance of the Rice Band.

The lakes of Stearns and Benton counties became recreation spots for fishing and swimming. Wooded areas and fields were used for hunting a wide array of wildlife, a proud example of which is captured in a memorable photograph of brothers August and Frank Bohm, posing with their successful hunt.

Torah (Richmond) baseball team, circa 1905. *Courtesy Stearns History Museum 12,473*

Orchestra in Rice, 1898. Left to right: Herman Fromelt, O.C. Greene, Golden Greene, and William Christl. *Courtesy Benton County Historical Society*

St. Joseph Coronet Band, circa 1895. *Courtesy Darol Studer*

St. Anthony Brass Band, circa 1895. First from the left with an instrument is Bernard Blume, fourth is John Gresser, and fifth is Theodore Vos; others unidentified. *Courtesy Stearns History Museum 14,525*

Rice band on July 4, 1895. Left to right: Slim McNeal, August Goumnitz, Leman Cairns, Norm McNeal, Ruben Chaser, Julius Momberg, Math Klein, Tony Rajkowski, Allie Gates, Herman Fromelt, Marsh McNeal, and George Sauer, Sr. *Courtesy Benton County Historical Society*

1906 Foley High School baseball team. Included in picture: Joseph Mushel, John E. Kasner, Benedict Mushel, and Ray Latterall.
Courtesy Benton County Historical Society

Cold Spring baseball team, 1910. Front row, left to right: Joe Peters, unknown, bat boy Richard Breen, Charles Gilley, and unknown. Middle row: John Gilley, Math Sauer, and Henry Miller. Back row is unknown. *Courtesy Stearns History Museum 11,012*

Torah baseball team, circa 1909. Back row, left to right: Albert Lang, Jacob Willenbring, John Butala, Jake Lemm, and Ray Wenck. Middle row: Ed Wurst, Gus Utecht, and Steve Braun. Front: Anton "Duke" Fuecker, and Mike Butala. *Courtesy Stearns History Museum 12,475*

Perkins Land Company baseball team, circa 1915. Back row, left to right: Frank Wisniewski, Anthony Kasner, and Frank Grosnick. Middle row: unknown, unknown, unknown, Joseph Mushel, unknown. Front row: John Kasner, unknown, Roy Latterell, Ben Mushel, and unknown. Sitting in front: Felix Mushel. *Courtesy Benton County Historical Society 864*

Sauk Rapids baseball team in 1911. *Courtesy Benton County Historical Society*

Amateur baseball team from St. Joseph, circa 1925. Top row, left to right: Nick Horsch, Christie Pallansch, coach Carl Lodermeier, Al Zapf, ___ Knifkowski. Bottom row: Spotsy Reber, Mike Pfannenstein, Wheezy Linneman, Ed Pfannenstein, Al Pfannenstein, Pete Speiser, and Matty Jost, batboy. *Courtesy Stearns History Museum 2811*

Cathedral High School football squad, 1923. Back row on the left is the coach, William (Duke) Wimmer. Back row on the right is Fr. Laurer, manager. Members of the squad included: __ Vradenburg, __ Lies, F. Fritz, R. Bartholemy, L. Hall, P. Steichen, J. Forcier, F. Gross, L. Mohs, F. Lacher, J. Kujawa, and H. Hollern. Subs included: Lies, Wedle, Collins, Schwinghammer, Schumacher, Kelly, and Mertes. This was the first football team since 1915. *Courtesy Tannis Gruber*

August Bohm, left, and his brother, Frank, toasting their successful hunt with their dog Barney at Popple Creek, Minden Township, Benton County, 1899. *Courtesy Roger Bohm*

Louis Lezen, August Rogesheske, Dutch Kutzurik, and an unidentified man of Sauk Rapids, circa 1910. *Courtesy Benton County Historical Society*

Tom Venstra on the shore of Grand Lake, circa 1925. *Courtesy Gloriann Ziebol*

Sauk Rapids City Band, 1905. Band members include: R. Leyerly, H. Grant, George Hohman, W. Miller, H. Heinzel, C. Roth, C. Sheldon, C. Peterson, _ Harland, William Scherbert, Harry Westcott, L. Sovereign, M. Sheldon, L. Miller, August Heinzel, J. Hohman, J. Berglund, E. Kuehl, and Frank Heinzel.
Courtesy Benton County Historical Society

SPORTS & LEISURE ❖ Page 117

Stage of Old Maurin Opera House, Cold Spring, circa 1910. *Courtesy Stearns History Museum 8,753*

Boys Band in front of Stearns County Courthouse, circa 1926. There were 240 boys in the organization and 202 are in the photo. G. Oliver Riggs was the bandmaster. *Courtesy Stearns History Museum 12,479*

Christine Netter working as hat check at the Wagon Wheel Supper Club in Waite Park, 1944. *Courtesy Dannielle Bunting*

Christine Netter on the Mississippi River bridge in St. Cloud, 1940. *Courtesy Dannielle Bunting*

Stearns County men standing around a wooden keg with a metal tap, circa 1930. The first man is Joe Fiala; others unidentified. *Courtesy Gloriann Ziebol*

Martin Eltrich with his bicycle, circa 1910. *Courtesy Gloriann Ziebol*

Model T Derby at the Benton County Fairgrounds, circa 1936. *Courtesy Stearns History Museum 7998*

St. Cloud Cathedral basketball team, 1929. *Courtesy Stearns History Museum 6,669*

Whistle basketball team sponsored by Bernick's Dr. Pepper Bottling Company in 1945. The team was named after a soft drink produced by Bernick's Bottling Company. *Courtesy James Gammell*

SPORTS & LEISURE ❖ Page 121

Hal Schadt signing autographs for St. Cloud Rox fans, circa 1946. *Courtesy Stearns History Museum - Myron Hall Collection*

St. Cloud Rox, 1947. *Courtesy Stearns History Museum - Myron Hall Collection*

Rox Stadium, circa 1949. *Courtesy Stearns History Museum - Myron Hall Collection*

St. Cloud Rox, May 4, 1948. Front row, left to right: Ray Coles, Ted Drakos, John Caufield, Corson Proctor, and Lee Wolters. Middle row: Del Burke, Joe Kelley, Nick Chanaka, Walt Stenborg, Ray Kott, and Charles Bernardi. Back row: Rance Pless, Jack Jonreau, manager Charley Fox, George Roden, Leonard Posciak, and Dick Bixby. *Courtesy Stearns History Museum - Myron Hall Collection*

EVENTS

Events of both celebratory and catastrophic natures helped shape what Stearns and Benton counties have become today.

Parades, festivals, winter carnivals, and other events were some of the positive ways communities would join together in celebration of a holiday, to pay tribute to the return of a hometown war hero or to recognize a local achievement. It is with these celebrations where civic pride flourished, strangers became lifelong friends and traditions were born.

Unfortunately some of the most memorable events are often the most horrific. Forces of nature and their destructive aftermath were no strangers to Central Minnesota. The tornado of 1886 ravaged most of Sauk Rapids, destroying almost every business and claiming 38 lives. The damage of the tornado was so severe and widespread that Sauk Rapids was no longer the dominant town and St. Cloud grew to become the main city of Central Minnesota.

Other tragedies such as fires claimed many homes, businesses and other buildings, resulting in the loss of an integral part of the footprint of early Stearns and Benton counties.

Sauk Rapids Fourth of July parade float in 1914. Edward Kutzorick is the driver; others unidentified. *Courtesy Benton County Historical Society 935*

Circus parade down St. Germain Street looking east, July 27, 1899. *Courtesy Stearns History Museum 8317*

Celebration on Main Street, Richmond, circa 1910. *Courtesy Stearns History Museum 7995*

A welcome home celebration after WW I taken in front of the Breen Hotel on St. Germain Street in St. Cloud, 1919. *Courtesy Mildred Burnett*

Parade on the 800 and 900 blocks of St. Germain Street looking west, August 24, 1928. *Courtesy Stearns History Museum 1795*

Sauk Rapids depot looking west after a tornado on April 14, 1886. In Sauk Rapids, the tornado destroyed the Benton County Courthouse, the church, school, post office, newspaper, and hotels. The storm leveled almost every business leaving 38 dead. Fortunately the school was not in session due to budget cuts. The building was totally destroyed along with over 100 other buildings. Following the storm, special trains brought doctors from St. Paul and help from communities between St. Cloud and Fergus Falls. As a result of the tornado, Sauk Rapids was no longer the dominant town in Central Minnesota and St. Cloud grew to take its place. *Courtesy Benton County Historical Society*

Broadway Avenue in Sauk Rapids after a tornado on April 14, 1886. The storm began about 4:00 p.m. southwest of St. Cloud and destroyed the bridge across the Mississippi River as it headed toward Sauk Rapids where it destroyed much of the community. *Courtesy Benton County Historical Society 695*

Woods Mill in Foley burned on June 15, 1909. *Courtesy Benton County Historical Society*

Fire at Davidson Opera House, 5th Avenue South in St. Cloud, February 5, 1913. *Courtesy Stearns History Museum 16,286*

Immaculate Conception Church in St. Cloud burned in 1920. *Courtesy Darol Studer*

Fire at the Clark Granite Company, Rockville, June 9, 1946. *Courtesy Stearns History Museum 12,255*

A fire started by a firecracker destroyed Strand Paint Shop and Prom Body Shop at 112 6th Avenue South, June 13, 1948. *Courtesy Lois Lunemann*

Progressive Farmers' Club's entry into the Harvest Festival in St. Cloud, circa 1930. On the left is Bernard H. Otte, next to him is Ole Halvorson, and on the far right is Ray Walker; others unidentified. *Courtesy Stearns History Museum 12,828*

Bernick's Dr. Pepper Bottling Company Christmas party, 1945. Francis Bernick is behind Santa with the white shirt and tie and Santa is James Gammell. *Courtesy James Gammell*

A meal served during Quality Milk and Egg Show in the St. Cloud Armory, February 15, 1949. *Courtesy Stearns History Museum 12,858*

Twenty-three people from St. Cloud went on a goodwill trip to visit Mellrichstadt, a town in Bavaria adopted by St. Cloud, June 1949. The group was led by Mayor Mathew Malisheski. The project was suggested by St. Cloud newspaper publisher Anton Volkmuth and over five tons of food was sent to Mellrichstadt. *Courtesy Bob and MaryAnn Malisheski*

St. Cloud East Side Boosters Club packaging Christmas bags in Bines Laundry, 1946. Right to left: Dick Varner, Butcher Shop; unknown, owner of Scenic Sign; Axel Anderson, Chief of Police; Hillis Meyer, Culligan Softener Service; Oscar Edwards, Edwards Grocery; Eddie Simmers, East Side Laundry; Emmett (Red) Schepers, Red's Cafe; Arnie Bines, partner of Eddie Simmers in East Side Laundry; unknown; and Clarence Horst, Lakeland Bakery. *Courtesy Penny Bergstaser*

St. Cloud parade, circa 1930. *Courtesy Stearns History Museum 7885*